The Best Little Bullfrog in the Forest

by Ian Whybrow
illustrated by Natalie Smillie

CAMBRIDGE
UNIVERSITY PRESS

UCL
Institute of Education

In the damp leaves on the floor of the forest, a little brown bullfrog sat with his mother. They were watching a talent contest.

'Can I be in it?' he asked.

'You're too little and too ugly!'
called Crested Cockatoo from up in a tree.

'You have lumpy brown skin! Not like
my beautiful feathers.
I am going to win the talent contest!'

'Don't listen,' said his mother.
'He's showing off.
You have lovely skin. Come on, let's go
and find somewhere cool.'

As they hopped through the forest,
a green parrot with a big red beak
flew past and sat on a branch.

'Look at that!' said the little bullfrog.
'I wish I could fly!'

'I am the best at flying,'
cried Great-Billed Parrot.

'My green and blue feathers are beautiful
and my big bill is strong.
I am going to win the talent contest!'

'I wish I was best at something,'
said the little bullfrog with a sigh.

'Don't be upset,' croaked his mother.
'Let's find somewhere cool.'

They had not gone far when they found
some doves singing.

'Can I join in?' asked the little bullfrog.
'I can sing.'

The little bullfrog croaked a song.

'What a horrible noise!' cooed a Zebra Dove, up in the branches. 'Listen to **me**. Now, that **is** a sweet song.'

'Listen to **my** song,' called Spotted Dove.

'It is much sweeter!

I am going to win the talent contest!'

And off they flew.

The little bullfrog was very upset.
'It's true,' he said.

'My song sounds like a burp.'

'You have a lovely voice,' said his mother.

'Come along. Let's go and catch some flies at the pool.'

They had a swim and ate some bugs.

Just then, White-lipped Pit-viper
came slithering towards them!

'Look out!' croaked Mother. 'Dive!'

Quick as a flash, they swam
to the bottom of the pool.
They were safe!

'I missed them! Where did they go?
I can't believe it! I am the fastest snake
in the forest!' he hissed to himself.

Suddenly there was an even louder hiss from a much bigger snake. It was Spitting Cobra!

'You're not the fastest!' he hissed.
'I can slither faster than you any day!
Watch me. Ready, steady, go!'

And with that, they slithered away.

The little brown bullfrog popped up in the water.

'Wow!' he gasped. 'They are nasty.'

Civet Cat was sleeping under a bush.
All the noise woke her up.

'Not as nasty as this,' she said, and let out
a very nasty smell. 'I can scare off
lots of animals with my smell.'

'That is disgusting!' said the little bullfrog.
'I wish I could make smells like that!'

Just then, the ground shook and, with a hiss louder than any snake, Komodo Dragon charged towards them.

'I'll show you disgusting!' he roared.

His smell was worse than Civet Cat's.

Komodo Dragon flicked his tongue
and with a swish of his mighty tail,
he bashed Civet Cat into the air.

Then he opened his horrible jaws
and gobbled her up.

'Oh no!' said the little bullfrog. 'I'm not best at anything.'

'I can't fly like Parrot and Cockatoo.
I can't sing like the doves.
I am not fast like the snakes.
I don't stink like Civet Cat.
I'm not disgusting like Komodo Dragon.
Tell me one thing that I'm the best at!'

'Well, you escaped from the snakes, Civet Cat and Komodo Dragon,' said his mother.
'You are the best at not getting eaten.
You are just the right colour to hide from your enemies in the leaf litter.
You are the best at hiding.
You can swim and dive under water.
You are the best at saving your skin.'

'Hey! That's true,' said the little bullfrog.

'And when you sing, I know exactly who you are and where you are. You are the best little bullfrog in the forest.'

Suddenly the little bullfrog felt very special.

The Best Little Bullfrog in the Forest ❧ Ian Whybrow

Teaching notes written by Sue Bodman and Glen Franklin

Using this book

Developing reading comprehension

This humorous story focuses on a little bullfrog who wants to be the best at something. The animals of the forest compete with each other at a talent contest and the little bullfrog is left feeling disheartened. The reader needs to understand why little bullfrog tries to compete and why his mother seems unconcerned that he isn't beautiful and can't sing. The vocabulary is chosen to help the reader gain inference, particularly that around the animal characters.

Grammar and sentence structure

- Amount of direct speech requiring use of punctuation to read fluently and with expression.
- Literary phrase; 'and' 'with' 'that'.

Word meaning and spelling

- Challenging vocabulary; 'slithering', 'charged', 'flicked', 'mighty'
- Decoding novel words in context: 'swish'
- Final y in adjectives; 'lumpy', 'ugly', 'nasty', 'mighty', 'smelly'.

Curriculum links

Science and nature – This story lends itself to links with project work on animals. The animals in the story have a range of talents and abilities. Pupils could use non-fiction texts to create profiles of their favourite animals, describing what each animal can do. This would enable pupils to experience the differences between writing fiction and non-fiction texts.

Further reading in this series that would like to this story includes; 'Big Bugs'; 'Life on the Reef'; 'Giants of the Ocean'.

Learning outcomes

Children can:

- search for and use familiar syllables within words to read longer words
- read longer phrases and more complex sentences
- attend to a greater range of punctuation and text layout.

A guided reading lesson

Book Introduction

Give each child a copy of the book and read the title

Orientation

In this story, the little bullfrog so wants to be the best at something. He can compete with the other animals when it comes to singing, flying, looking beautiful - or even being smelly and disgusting. But of course, his mother loves him best of all and wouldn't want him any other way. Give a brief orientation to the text: *This story is called 'The Best Little Bullfrog in the Forest'. What do you think the little bullfrog could be best at?*

Preparation

As you prepare this text, make sure that you model and rehearse the names of any animals that the children are unfamiliar with.

Pages 2 and 3: There is a talent contest going on in the forest and the little bullfrog wants to be in it. What sorts of things do you think the animals will do to try to win? Gather ideas about the skills and talents that the animals might display. *Yes, they might try and sing, or fly or look beautiful – let's look through the pages to see who will try and win the talent contest.*

Continue through the book focussing discussion on what each animal might do to try and win the talent contest